THIS BOOK BELONGS TO

YOU DON'T HAVE TO BE CRAZY TO WORK HERE WE WILL TRAIN YOU

PEOPLE I WANT TO PUNCH IN THE FACE

THANK YOU FOR BEING A SUPER AWESOME TEAM BEST TEAM EVER

EVERYONE WAS THINKING IT I JUST SAID IT

NOTES FROM ANOTHER MEETING THAT SHOULD HAVE BEEN AN EMAIL

I MAY LOOK LIKE I'M DOING NOTHING BUT IN MY HEAD I'M QUITE BUSY

SHIT I NEED TO REMEMBER

THANK YOU FOR THE AMAZING JOB YOU DO EVERY DAY!

I'M SO GOOD AT MY JOB, OTHERS WANT ME TO DO THEIR JOB TOO

PEOPLE SHOULD SERIOUSLY STOP EXPECTING NORMAL FROM ME

THEY SAID DON'T GIVE UP ON YOUR DREAMS. SO I WENT BACK TO SLEEP

EVERY ONCE IN A WHILE SOMEONE AMAZING COMES ALONG...AND HERE I AM

I GET THROUGH MONDAYS BY CONVINCING MYSELF I'LL QUIT ON FRIDAY

I SURVIVED ANOTHER MEETING THAT SHOULD HAVE BEEN AN EMAIL

I WORK HARD SO MY CAT CAN HAVE A BETTER LIFE

IT'S OK IF YOU DISAGREE WITH ME. I CAN'T FORCE YOU TO BE RIGHT

MY GREAT IDEAS THAT SOMEONE ELSE WILL TAKE THE CREDIT FOR

MY OPINION OFFENDED YOU? YOU SHOULD HEAR WHAT I KEEP TO MYSELF

SURE, LET ME DROP EVERYTHING AND WORK ON YOUR PROBLEM

I DON'T HAVE ENOUGH MIDDLE FINGERS FOR TODAY

LOOK AT YOU GETTING PROMOTED AND SHIT

SORRY I CAN'T HEAR YOU OVER THE SOUND OF HOW AWESOME I AM

HOLD ON LET ME OVERTHINK THIS

UNDERESTIMATE ME. THAT'LL BE FUN

SOME DAYS, THE BEST THING ABOUT MY JOB IS THAT THE CHAIR SPINS

MY PEOPLE SKILLS ARE JUST FINE. IT'S MY TOLERANCE TO IDIOTS THAT NEEDS WORK

YOU'RE STILL SOBER. KEEP THAT SHIT UP

I KNOW I'M YOUR FAVORITE EMPLOYEE. I MEAN LOOK AROUND...

BOSS BECAUSE FREAKING BADASS IS NOT AN OFFICIAL JOB TITLE

HUMAN RESOURCES BECAUSE FREAKING MIRACLE WORKER IS NOT AN OFFICIAL JOB TITLE

ADMIN PROFESSIONAL BECAUSE FREAKING AWESOME IS NOT AN OFFICIAL JOB TITLE

I WORK WELL WITH OTHERS WHEN THEY LEAVE ME ALONE

Printed in Great Britain
by Amazon

14735427R00068